SLIP STREAM

BIZARRE BUILDINGS

ANNE ROONEY

NEGATIVE 35 mm

35   36

EDGE

D0258845

First published in 2014 by
Franklin Watts
338 Euston Road
London NW1 3BH

Franklin Watts Australia
Level 17/207 Kent Street
Sydney NSW 2000

© Franklin Watts 2013

(ebook) ISBN: 978 1 4451 2904 4
(pb) ISBN 978 1 4451 3229 7
(library ebook) ISBN: 978 1 4451 2506 0

Dewey classification number: 720

The right of Anne Rooney to be
identified as the author of this Work
has been asserted in accordance
with the Copyright, Designs and
Patents Act, 1988.

A CIP catalogue record for this book is
available from the British Library.

Series Editors: Adrian Cole and Jackie Hamley
Series Advisors: Diana Bentley and Dee Reid
Series Designer: Peter Scoulding
Picture Researcher: Diana Morris

Printed in China

Franklin Watts is a division of
Hachette Children's Books,
an Hachette UK company.
www.hachette.co.uk

Acknowledgements:
Alamy Celebrity/Alamy: 10, 11.
Marcel Antonisse/epa/Corbis: 20.
Mark Burnett/Alamy: 6.
Pat Canova/Alamy: front cover, 5.
Charles O. Cecil/Alamy: 17.
Leonhard Foeger/Corbis: 22, 23.
Fotoeye75/Dreamstime: 19.
James Kirkikis/Alamy: 7.
Leontura/istockphoto: 4-5b.
Elisa Locci/istockphoto: 14.
LOOK Die Bildagentur der Fotografen
GmbH/Alamy: 16.
Olaf Loose/istockphoto: 1.
José Marafona/Dreamstime: 12.
Wayne McKown/Dreamstime: 18.
Nippel/ istockphoto: 9.
E.Pais/ Shutterstock: 4cr, 21.
Daniel Rosenbaum/istockphoto: 15.
Shutterstock: 4cl, 8.
Design: Tham & Videgård Architects.
Photo: Peter Lundstrom, WDO – www.
mirrorcube.se: 13.

Every attempt has been made to
clear copyright. Should there be any
inadvertent omission, please apply
to the publisher for rectification.

CONTENTS

BIZARRE BUILDINGS

There are some very odd buildings in the world.
Some don't even look like buildings.

How would you like to live upside-down? This building in Florida, USA, looks as if it has been dropped.

IT LOOKS LIKE...

This building is called the Longaberger Basket in Ohio, USA. Can you guess what the firm makes?

THE LORD OF THE RINGS

J.R.R. TOLKIEN

A TALE OF TWO CITIES

CHARLES DICKENS

Charlotte's Web

E.B.

ROMEO AND JULIET

William Shakes

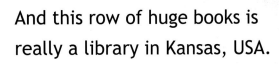

And this row of huge books is really a library in Kansas, USA.

GIANT CRYSTAL

The Atomium in Brussels, Belgium is a model of an iron crystal. It is 165 billion times bigger than an iron crystal really is.

Escalators in the tunnels link the round rooms.

CHINESE GIANTS

The Tianzi Hotel in China looks like three men. They are three Chinese gods called Fu, Lu and Shou. They stand for happiness, good luck and long life.

STICKS AND STONES

The Stone House in Portugal is built beside a huge rock. It looks as if the rock has rolled into the house.

This tree house in Sweden is hard to see. It is covered in mirrors.

A COLD PLACE TO STAY

This hotel in Sweden is made entirely from ice. Even the beds are cut from blocks of ice! Every summer, the hotel melts. It is made again each winter.

ANIMAL FRIENDS

This building looks like a giant sheep. It is the Big Sheep Wool Gallery in New Zealand. It sells things made of wool. It is next to...

...the Big Dog Tourist Office!

BROKEN BUILDING

Believe it or not - a building ripped in half! This building is in Missouri, USA. It belongs to a company called Ripley. They make a series of books called "Believe it or Not".

BODY MUSEUM

The Corpus Museum in Holland looks like a person. 'Corpus' means body. It is a museum about the human body.

Some of the rooms in the building look like the insides of a body.

OOPS!

It looks as if the little house has been thrown at the big building and got stuck! This odd pair of buildings is in Vienna, Austria.

INDEX

FOR TEACHERS

About
SLIPSTREAM

Slipstream is a series of expertly levelled books designed for pupils who are struggling with reading. Its unique three-strand approach through fiction, graphic fiction and non-fiction gives pupils a rich reading experience that will accelerate their progress and close the reading gap.

At the heart of every Slipstream non-fiction book is exciting information. Easily accessible words and phrases ensure that pupils both decode and comprehend, and the topics really engage older struggling readers.

Whether you're using Slipstream Level 2 for Guided Reading or as an independent read, here are some suggestions:

1. Make each reading session successful. Talk about the text before the pupil starts reading. Introduce any unfamiliar vocabulary.

2. Encourage the pupil to talk about the book using a range of open questions. For example, what strange building would they design? What would it be used for?

3. Discuss the differences between reading non-fiction, fiction and graphic fiction. Which do they prefer?

For guidance, SLIPSTREAM Level 2 – Bizarre Buildings has been approximately measured to:

National Curriculum Level: 2b
Reading Age: 7.6–8.0
Book Band: Purple

ATOS: 2.4
Guided Reading Level: I
Lexile® Measure (confirmed): 570L

Slipstream Level 2 photocopiable **WORKBOOK**
ISBN: 978 1 4451 1797 3
available – download free sample worksheets from:
www.franklinwatts.co.uk